**LAYING UP TREASURE
IN THE LAST DAYS**

*The Distinct Eschatology
of the Epistle of James*

Brian Stanley Douglas

Copyright 2019, Brian Stanley Douglas. All rights reserved.

Print ISBN: 978-0-578-43592-3

ebook ISBN: 978-0-578-43593-0

All biblical quotations are from the English Standard Version.

To my daughter, Mila

I hope you will always love books

While the Epistle of James is one of the most unique and instructive books in the New Testament, it is also one of the most difficult to categorize. Few doubt the wisdom of the letter's instruction in living the Christian life, or its insight into the perspectives, persecutions, and struggles of the early church. Nevertheless, there are a wide divergence of opinions about its purpose and usefulness within the canon of Scripture.

Some see James as the New Testament equivalent to some section of the Old Testament: Law,[1] Poetry,[2] or Prophecy.[3] Many scholars have pointed out

---

[1] Merrill F. Unger, *Unger's Bible Handbook* (Chicago: Moody, 1975), 783.

[2] Ryken, Wilhoit, and Longman, eds., *Dictionary of Biblical Imagery* (Downers Grove, Ill: InterVarsity, 1998), 434.

[3] James B. Adamson, *The Epistle of James*, The New International Commentary on the New Testament (Grand Rapids: William B.

a connection between the book of James and Jesus' Sermon on the Mount.[4] Some describe it as a distinctly Jewish book,[5] while others declare its style to be that of a Greco-Roman letter.[6] Martin Luther's initial disapproval of James is well-known. These perspectives are, of course, not mutually exclusive, but James has long tended to confound its interpreters about its author's

---

Eerdmans, 1979), 20; Elwell and Yarbrough, *Encountering the New Testament* (Grand Rapids: Baker, 1998), 355.

[4] Raymond Brown, *An Introduction to the New Testament* (New York: Doubleday, 1997), 734-735; Robert H. Gundry, *A Survey of the New Testament* (Grand Rapids: Zondervan, 1994), 434; Adamson, 20f, 147f; Elwell and Yarbrough, 356, 358; Unger, 783.

[5] Gundry, *Survey*, 434; Unger, 783. For a particularly pointed perspective on the epistle's Jewish character, see Robert H. Gundry, *Commentary on James* (Grand Rapids: Baker Academic, 2010).

[6] See Todd C. Penner, *The Epistle of James and Eschatology* (Sheffield: Sheffield Academic Press, 1996), 122ff.

design in writing it.

This booklet is a concise examination of James with different categories than those above. Here we will suggest that readers of James's epistle should understand its underlying purpose as essentially *eschatological*: this letter was written to be a practical guide for Christian life *in the last days*. This underlying eschatological purpose is demonstrated by the epistle's structure and themes.

I. THE ESCHATOLOGICAL STRUCTURE OF JAMES

Many commentators regard James as a thematically disorganized book. One described it as a "series of loosely related homilies,"[7] another deemed it "difficult to outline" because of its "rambling and monastic style,"[8] and still another says its structure has "led many to throw up their hands in despair over finding any unity in the book."[9] Some believe James seems so disjointed because the existing form is a redacted version of the original

---

[7] Carson, Moo, and Morris, *An Introduction to the New Testament* (Grand Rapids: Zondervan, 1992), 409.
[8] Gundry, *Survey*, 434.
[9] Peter H. Davids, *The Epistle of James*, New International Greek Testament Commentary (Grand Rapids: William B. Eerdmans, 1983), 22.

document.[10, 11]

However, no one should discount the literary quality of James simply because it does not follow an obvious, logically progressive outline. As the *Dictionary of Biblical Imagery* describes the epistle's literary virtue: "The epistle of James, though written in prose, is so laden with images and metaphors that it ranks as poetic prose."[12]

Far from being a disorganized collection of independent thoughts, James is instead a beautiful, fugue-like intertwining of several themes. Each one is brought to prominence for a moment, then

---

[10] Brown, 734; Davids, 22.

[11] For a helpful, concise summary of the several proposed structural analyses of James, see Craig L. Blomberg and Mariam J. Kamell, *James*, Zondervan Exegetical Commentary on the New Testament (Grand Rapids: Zondervan, 2008), 22-27.

[12] Ryken, et al, 434.

covered by another for a time before later resurfacing.

In addition, James demonstrates a distinct outline, which will be demonstrated below. This structure and each intertwined theme ultimately direct the reader to the epistle's central message, which is distinctly eschatological: Christians are to remain steadfast so that they may receive "the crown of life, which God has promised to those who love him" (1:12), for "the Lord is compassionate and merciful" (5.11).

The centrality of eschatology is emphasized by the epistle's overall structure. Penner considers the eschatological character of James's framework to be "clearly evident" and outlines the book as follows:[13]

---

[13] Penner, 211.

a - epistle prologue (1:1)

b - opening section (1:2-12)

c - main body (1:13-4:5)

b¹ - closing section (4:6-5:12)

a¹ - epistle conclusion (5:13-20)

The Epistle Prologue and Conclusion

The epistle prologue and conclusion most explicitly display the author's "last days" outlook. In the prologue (1:1), James identifies himself as a "servant of God and of the Lord Jesus Christ," and he addresses his letter "to the twelve tribes in the Dispersion."

James was a Jew and a leader in the primarily Jewish church at Jerusalem, and he was writing to Christ-believing Jews (2:1) who had been scattered throughout the Roman Empire. Judging by the letter's content, these Christian Jews were being oppressed severely. James wrote often of encouragement and perseverance (1:2-4, 12, 17-21, 27; 2:12; 3:18; 4:6-10; 5:7ff), and yet he made no reference to any period or relief or any re-gathering of Israel between the present age and the age to come—the thought seems to have never entered his mind. In fact, he taught that the current state of things would continue until the return of the Lord (5:7-8). James "sees the church standing at the end of history. The tension between this age and the age to come is high. The inbreaking of the new age is imminent."[14]

Similarly, James concluded his letter with an appeal of eschatological significance. He encouraged his fellow believers to do anything they can to restore those who have wandered from the truth, reminding them that in light of the coming end to the present age, their very souls are on the line (5:19-20). James's final words are weighty, emphasizing the ultimate nature of the believer's present actions: "Whoever turns a sinner from the error of their way will save them from death and cover over a multitude of sins."

---

[14] Davids, 38.

The Opening and Closing Sections

In the words of Todd C. Penner, "The importance of the body opening… is that it introduces the material which is to be laid out in the main part of the letter"; it "lays the foundation… from which the superstructure may grow."[15]

While the extent of the opening section is disputed among scholars,[16] wherever one draws its boundaries, the opening section has a clear eschatological character. James commands his readers to be joyful in trials (1:2) because those who persevere until the end are promised full sanctification (1:4). He assures them that their oppressors will meet their end (1:11) and that those who love God will receive a

---

[15] Penner argues from a chiastic structure that the opening section is 1:2-12. Penner, 143.
[16] Ibid, 145.

great reward (1:12). These eschatological thoughts provide the foundation for the rest of the Epistle.

Penner again argues from a chiastic structure that 4:6-5:12 serves as the closing section of the Epistle.[17] Like the opening section, the focus of James's last words is distinctly eschatological: James writes of God's future exaltation of the humble (4:10), the one lawgiver and judge (4:12), the foolishness of living as if there will be no end or judgment (4:13-16), the miseries that are coming upon the oppressors (5:1) because of their sins (5:4-6), the judgment that is already upon them (5:2-3), the imminence of the Lord's return (5:7-8), and the promise of mercy for those who remain steadfast (5:11).

---

[17] Ibid, 157.

The eschatological motifs of the letter's opening and closing sections are strikingly parallel:[18]

1. The need for steadfastness and patience in light of God's imminent return (1:2-4, 12 and 5:7-12).

2. The nature and character of that steadfastness (1:2-8 and 4:7-12; 5:7-12).

3. The importance of avoiding double-mindedness and duplicity in one's relationship with God because of the eternal stakes (1:5-8 and 4:7-10).

---

[18] The following list is adapted from Penner, 211.

4. God's ultimate judgment of all men (1:9-11 and 4:6, 13-17; 5:1-6).

5. The exaltation of the poor and the humiliation of the rich at the time of judgment (1:9-11 and 4:6-5:6).

The Main Body

The opening and closing sections "are intended to frame the main body of James 1:13-4:5, and [this] device was consciously utilized by the writer of the epistle."[19] James intended for his readers to understand the practical teachings of the Epistle's main body on the basis of the foundational eschatological truths of the opening and closing sections. Therefore, the structure of the letter demonstrates its purpose: the Epistle of James was written as a practical guide for Christian life in the last days.

With James's structure in mind, let us consider how three of the epistle's main themes are eschatological in nature.

---

[19] Ibid.

II. THE ESCHATOLOGICAL THEMES OF JAMES

Davids correctly asserts that eschatology is not the *message* of James, but rather is the *context* in which its message is found. As an example of how this concept shapes our understanding of James, he writes, "Without an appreciation of the foundational role [eschatology] played in the Christian world view of James's church, one could hardly understand the joy referred to in 1:2, 12."[20]

This same idea applies to the central themes of the Epistle: they cannot be fully understood without placing them in their eschatological context. Interestingly, the letter's main eschatological themes can be grouped into three contrasting pairs.

---

[20] Davids, 39.

God versus the Enemies of God

One of the central themes in James is his doctrine of God. God is mentioned often, with his dominion over the world at the forefront in each instance.

God is the never-changing sovereign over all things (1:17b). He is the only lawgiver (4:12), and his law is royal, ruling over everyone (2:8). He is the only judge (4:12), and all men will be judged according to his law (2:12-13). He is the giver of every perfect gift (1:17), but he is able to save and to destroy as he pleases (4:12). He hears the cries of the innocent (5:4) and every word that comes from the mouth of man, even the oaths he takes (5:12), and will respond to them with justice. The God of James is clearly a Ruler-Judge. Indeed, one of James's most ominous warnings is that "the Judge is standing at the door" (5:9)—his justice is imminent.

Pitted against God in James is the demonic realm, which shudders at the very thought of His existence and nature (2:19) and whose thinking is directly opposed to His own (3:15). Further, the world itself is at enmity with God (4:4), and all who are in it who have not submitted themselves to God and resisted the demonic realm are in opposition to Him (4:7).

According to James, God is waging war against His enemies. That conflict is the cosmic background to what James wrote, and it is the greater context from which his eschatological understanding of the world emerges.

The Righteous versus the Evil

The war between God and His enemies is not just a battle between unseen spiritual forces, James argued. It is manifested among the peoples of the earth.

James described two kinds of people who participate in this conflict. The first: God has a people who love Him (1:12, 2:5). James characterizes them as the Righteous. They have kept the law (2:8, 3:2), they care about others (1:27, 2:8, 5:19-20), and are peacemakers, gentle, open to reason, full of mercy and good fruits, impartial, sincere (3:17-18), and wise (1:5-7, 3:13). The Righteous are further described as the humble (1:21, 3:13, 4:7-8, 10) and the poor (1:9, 2:15, 3:5, 5:4) of the earth.

One of the chief characteristics of the Righteous is their faith. Their faith is full confidence in God's promises (1:6) and repentance of past wandering away from the truth (5:20). Most importantly, however, their faith is made plain through their works (1:27, 2:14-26, 3:13-18). The book of James is famous for its insistence that true faith manifests itself in works consistent with the righteousness that belongs to the people of God.

Several "Righteous heroes" are mentioned throughout the Epistle: Abraham (2:21, 23), Rahab (2:25), the prophets (5:10) Job (5:11), and Elijah (5:17). Readers are encouraged to follow in their footsteps (5:10) and become, as Abraham was, a "friend of God" (2:23).

James contrasts a second group of people against the Righteous; he calls them the Evil. The two could not be more antithetical.

The Evil are uncontrolled (1:26, 3:5-8), adulterous (2:11), murderous (2:11,

5:6), blasphemous (2:7), partial (2:1, 9), proud and opposed to God (4:6), rebellious sinners (1:14, 4:8), bitterly jealous, selfishly ambitious, boasters, liars, disorderly, and engaged in "every vile practice" (3:14,16). They are double-minded in all they do (1:8, 23-24; 3:8; 4:8). They know what is right, but they do not do it (4:17). Because they are lured into sin by their own desires, they are bound for death (1:14). They violently oppress the righteous whenever possible (5:1-6), even though their power is fleeting (1:10-11, 4:14). Worst of all, they attempt to usurp of the Judge (2:4, 4:11-12, 5:6). The Evil anti-heroes boast of their plans to do their own will without any regard for God, His law, His people, or their impending judgment (4:13-5:1).

Through these descriptions, James demonstrates that the conflict between the Righteous and the Evil is the earthly manifestation of the cosmic conflict between God and His enemies. Every person is either among the Righteous or among the Evil, on the side of either God or His enemies. James knows no neutral position; he has drawn the proverbial line in the sand.

James appeals to God's immutability (1:17) and His ability to do whatever He wills as the grounds for hope for those who are with Him (1:18, 4:12) and the grounds for despair for those who are against Him (2:19, 3:16). But there is an even greater ground for hope or despair: the Judge will bring a complete and permanent justice in the end.

The Judgment of the Righteous versus the Evil

James makes it clear that the Ruler-Judge will bring justice for all the unjust acts of the Evil. They will fade away in the midst of their pursuits (1:11), he promises. Their very best attempt at saving faith is worthless (1:26). Their doom is so sure, in fact, that they should be weeping and howling even now because of the disasters that will overtake them (5:1). Their greatness and wealth are even now gone (5:2-3), for the Ruler-Judge has heard the case against them (5:4-6). Those who attempted to usurp the Ruler-Judge (2:4, 4:11-12, 5:6) will soon be destroyed by His justice. The Evil have genuine grounds for despair.

The Righteous will face the Ruler-Judge, too, James writes, but theirs will be a judgment of hope. Indeed, the Epistle is overflowing with calls for believers to act with their future judgment in mind and examples of how they must do that (e.g., 1:25, 2:12, etc).

Their wisest leaders—the teachers—will be judged "with greater strictness" (3:1). The Righteous are told to draw near to God, cleanse their hands, and purify their hearts. They must be wretched and mourn and weep; they must let their laughter be turned to mourning and their joy to gloom. But if they humble themselves before the God, James promises, then He will exalt them (4:8-10) and will surely make them perfect and complete (1:4). In fact, if they remain steadfast, they will be rewarded with the crown of life (1:12). Even more than that, James writes that God has chosen them to inherit His kingdom (2:5).

Judgment in James is invariably along those lines. Even though the Righteous are the poor and humble of the earth and the Evil are the rich and arrogant oppressors, God will raise the Righteous up to prominence above everything else on earth,[21] while the Evil will be brought to utter ruin. This judgment is imminent (5:8); that is the eschatological hope for the Righteous and should cause the Evil to despair.

In James's view, this judgment will take place at the time of the return of the Lord (5:7-8). The *parousia* is the trigger that will bring the promised justice to pass, and it is to that event that the believer anxiously looks and places his hope. At that time, not only will the Evil be humbled and the Righteous be exalted (1:9-11), but the

---

[21] This is an eschatological promise to restore the hierarchy of creation, with man over all the created realm – see Genesis 1:28-30.

conflict between God and His enemies will also be brought to an end. All corruption and strife will pass away and only what is righteous will remain (1:11, 15, 18; 2:13; 3:18; 4:1-4, 12; 5:19-20).

III. THE HEART OF JAMES'S ESCHATOLOGY

James's connection between the coming judgment and the second coming of Jesus is a thought common to the eschatology of every other New Testament writer.[22] The *parousia* and its concomitant events are the very centerpiece of New Testament eschatology.

But James, like other New Testament authors, appeals not only to future events when considering eschatology, but also to that which has *already occurred* as a guarantee that the promised future events will occur. In James's mind, the last days have *already begun*.

James tells the Righteous that they

---

[22] See Robert L. Reymond, *A New Systematic Theology of the Christian Faith* (Nashville: Thomas Nelson, 1998), 991-1066.

have *already* been "brought forth by the word of truth" according to the will of God (1:18). They have *already* been chosen to inherit the kingdom (2:5), and because they have *already* repented and received the implanted word of truth, their souls will be saved (1:18, 21; 5:20).

James's distinction between the judgment that has already happened and the judgment will yet happen can be found in his description of the plight of the Evil (5:1-6). He writes that judgment is coming upon them (5:1, 3) because of their sins (5:4-6), and yet *even now* their riches have rotted, their garments are moth-eaten, and their gold and silver have corroded (5:2-3). Future eschatological events are proven to be on their way by an examination of what has already happened—*even now* the effects of the destruction can be seen.

Most significantly, the Righteous have *already* been given, to one degree or another, a wisdom that is from above (3:13-18).

> As James makes clear in his 3rd chapter, there is wisdom from above for those who belong to Christ, a wisdom that is transcendent and of a different world. For those who belong to Christ and have been graciously brought in principle to the realm which is above, that eschatological wisdom is at work, conforming them to the image of Christ... True wisdom begins with that which is above, it is available for all who seek it, and it can never be displaced. True wisdom is not found in the earthly, but in the heavenly. It is found in that which is above (3:15)... Eschatological wisdom, then, speaks loudly to we who believe about living for the

Lord and not living for the riches of this life (5:1-3).[23]

Because of God's will and work (1:18), the Righteous are partakers of that wisdom. Their salvation has already begun, and its completion is assured (1:4, 3:18, 5:11). James's eschatological teaching is notably consistent with Paul's statement, "And I am sure of this, that he who began a good work in you will bring it to completion at the day of Jesus Christ" (Philippians 1:6).

James's own testimony as a Jew who is now a servant of the Lord Jesus Christ (1:1) indicates that he finds the origins of his "salvation already begun" in the work of Christ at the time of His first advent.

Indeed, the method and content of James's teaching is very similar to that of

---

[23] Danny Olinger, unpublished notes on redemptive-historical threads in James.

Jesus. Many scholars have pointed out a similarity between James's practical guide for Christian living and Jesus' Sermon on the Mount.[24] It is no surprise, then, that "James's eschatology is that which was promulgated by Jesus—an 'eschatological dualism' espousing both the 'already' of an 'inaugurated eschatology' and the 'not yet' of future cosmic eventualities."[25]

---

[24] See note 4 above.
[25] Reymond, 1009.

IV. A UNIQUE ESCHATOLOGICAL PERSPECTIVE

While James is a distinctly eschatological letter, it does not contain a distinct eschatology *per se* as its thought is not unique or innovative amongst the New Testament documents. As Gerald Bray described the general eschatological thought of the New Testament, "One of the most persuasive themes of the New Testament is that we are living in the 'last days' and that time will come to an end suddenly and without warning."[26]

> At [the end of time], the world would be judged and transformed into a kingdom fit for God. Believers in Christ are therefore

---

[26] Gerald Bray, *God is Love: A Biblical and Systematic Theology* (Wheaton: Crossway, 2012), 723.

encouraged to watch and to pray for that day to arrive. No one can say when Christ will return, but everyone is expected to be prepared for an event that could occur at any moment and catch us unawares. Those who are not ready for Christ's return will suffer the consequences, but those who are ready will inherit the kingdom that has been prepared for them from the foundation of the world.[27]

In terms of its eschatological system, James fits right in with the other New Testament books. This consistency with the rest of the New Testament is not surprising. However, it does highlight the epistle's one distinct eschatological contribution.

---

[27] Ibid, 729.

Perhaps the lone unique feature of James's eschatology is its sheer practicality. While all the New Testament is practically instructive, James is especially so. Virtually every commentator of every theological perspective, regardless of what particular angle they might take on the book itself, has pointed out the epistle's intensely pragmatic nature. Of the New Testament books, James is the writer most concerned about what Christians are to *do* in response to what Gerald Bray calls "the trials of the saved."[28] James uses imperatives more frequently than any other book in the Bible—over fifty imperatives in one hundred eight verses—demonstrating his desire to call God's people to action in light of the gospel.

It is less frequently noticed that James's intensely practical instruction is driven by his deep eschatological

---

[28] Bray, 726.

awareness. In accord with the eschatological dualism of the broader New Testament (as noted above), James repeatedly implores his readers to live in a manner consistent with the wisdom of which God has already made them partakers and will yet perfect them. Reymond aptly summarizes James's distinct purpose as a practical guide for Christian life in the last days:

> In sum, the Lord is coming and he is coming to judge the earth "by the [royal] law that gives freedom" (James 5:9; 2:8, 12-13). Christians, as heirs of the kingdom, are to look forward to the kingdom God has promised to those who love him (2:5). James employs his eschatology as a practical incentive for growth in holiness (see here in I

John 3:2-3; Rev. 22:17)![29]

Readers should also note the hopeful nature of the epistle's deeply practical nature. As Bray describes the eschatological hope of the New Testament documents,

> The material world will decay and disappear, but our life is neither hopeless or meaningless. What we do matters to God, and in the end it will be rewarded. As Paul put it, "The sufferings of this present time are not worth comparing with the glory that is to be revealed in us."[30]

When James instructs his readers—to count it all joy, ask for wisdom, be doers of the word, bridle their tongues, draw near to God, be patient until the coming of the Lord, lay up treasure in the

---

[29] Reymond, 1009.
[30] Bray, 729.

last days, and the like—he is pointing them toward that same eschatological hope of glory.

V. SUMMARY OF JAMES'S ESCHATOLOGY

1. The structure of James demonstrates it was written for an eschatological purpose.

2. Eschatology is not the *message* of the Epistle, but it is the *context* in which its message is presented.

3. The eschatological thematic context of James is one of conflict between God/the Righteous and God's enemies/the Evil.

4. That conflict will end with the return of the Lord Jesus Christ and the judgment of all men, both the Righteous and the Evil.

5. The victory of God and the Righteous is assured because of the work of Christ at His first advent and is evidenced by

rewards and judgments that are already being given out.

6. James teaches an eschatological dualism espousing both the "already" of an inaugurated eschatology and the "not yet" of future eschatological consummation.

7. In light of these eventualities, James admonishes believers to live in a manner consistent with the wisdom they have already been given.

ACKNOWLEDGEMENTS

Thank you to R. Fowler White, friend and former professor, in whose class this article began, many years ago;

To Charles Anderson, whose thorough feedback redirected this research at a crucial time;

And to Brad Chaney, friend and co-laborer, who provided helpful input along the way.

ABOUT THE AUTHOR

Brian Stanley Douglas lives in Boise, Idaho. He is husband to Jordan, father to three, pastor at All Saints Presbyterian Church, and chaplain at the Wyakin Foundation.

He formerly taught history, humanities, and political science and studied at Stetson University, Knox Seminary, Sussex University, and Boise State University. He is a soccer enthusiast, a lifelong fan of the Detroit Tigers, and a mediocre poet.

www.brianstanleydouglas.com

www.ingramcontent.com/pod-product-compliance
Lightning Source LLC
Chambersburg PA
CBHW022000290426
44108CB00012B/1153